Leadership,

a Practical Guide to

Theory and Practice

B. Charles Henry

Information Technology Manager & Adjunct Lecturer

Contents

Preface

Leadership is a highly debated topic in contemporary America and around the world. The mystery of leadership and in particular, good leadership has long been debated by respective civilizations for centuries. Respected authors throughout the history of modern man have posited many theories and new theories continue to emerge though scholarly and practical examination of hypotheses as modern societies search for new and improved ways of accomplishing effective leadership.

It has been argued and largely accepted that good leadership is not the purview of a specific brand or type of leadership but an amalgam of different leadership principles and practices. For example, leadership is not an issue of traits, dispositions, situations, and visions per say.

Instead, leadership is a combination of all such behaviors, attitudes, and characteristics. Good leadership therefore brings to the role of leadership a combination of the respective leadership principles depending on traits, behaviors, and the situation of prevailing circumstances.

Leadership must be recognize not so much as a group of followers and leaders independent of each other's duties and responsibilities, but must be seen as a relationship between leaders and followers. I proffer that it is the *relationship* that exists between leaders and followers that forms *leadership*.

Each section of the book stands alone. It is not therefore the intention of the author for the reader to read the book from cover to cover, though it is a light read and would not hinder understanding. The author's intention is to offer some practical guide to Leadership practice rather than to present a theoretical construct that reads like a novel from cover to cover. Enough of those exist. The objective here is to engage the reader to participate in the discourse and to make the transition from an academic discussion to implementation and management of one's leadership style.

Because the intention of the book is to provide guidance to the reader, I have followed each section immediately with its references for further probity and assessment of the argument presented without having to flip back and forth between the respective chapters and the back of the book. No additional reference pages are included.

The book is only a few pages of easy read and one hopes that there will be some enjoyment in sifting through the materials presented and that a lively discussion will ensue. I bid all readers a productive and engaging reading exercise. The book is also ideal for undergraduates and postgraduates pursuing a foundation information systems course or any introductory management or leadership courses.

Author's Biography

The author originates from Jamaica in the West Indies. He holds a Bachelor of Science degree with majors in Accounting and Management Studies and a Master's of Science degree in Computer Based Management Information Systems, both from the University of the West Indies, Mona campus in Kingston, Jamaica. The author is currently pursuing doctoral studies in Organizational Leadership with specialization in Information Systems and Technology.

The author is an Information Technology Manager and an Adjunct Lecturer in various information systems courses. The author achieved the Who's Who of Professionals recognition in 2001. In 2002, he was nominated a Mover and Shaker in the premier local daily newspaper. He is a full member of IEEE Computer Society

and a member of the Jamaica Computer Society.

1 Leadership Models

The phenomenon of leadership has fascinated and intrigued individuals for centuries and continues to do so today. Pharaoh, Aristotle, Jesus, Hitler, Stalin, Reagan, the Dalai Lama, Castro, and a host of others have influenced leadership. Whether such influences are positive or negative requires further analysis and interpretation. Although leadership has remained a necessary tool of engagement, motivation, and results, its precise role is not fully understood. Roles or impact of leadership is likely to be vague until scholars and practitioners alike accept a coherent, consistent, and agreed definition of leadership. The current set of definitions of leadership, too often, appears distant and may lead pursuers of leadership knowledge in varying directions.

A realistic definition of leadership comes from Baas (as cited in Wren, 1995) that stated:

> ... Leadership has been conceived as the focus of group processes, as a matter of personality, as a matter of inducing compliance, as the exercise of influence, as particular behaviors, ... as initiation of structure, and as many combinations of these definitions (p. 38).

Notwithstanding the plethora of definitions, scholars agree that leadership is comprised of leaders, followers, and situations. Hersey and Blanchard (as cited in Wren, 1995) noted, "Successful leaders are those who can adapt their leader behavior to meet the needs of their followers and the particular situation" (p. 148). Inherent in the quote is that leaders cannot exist without followers. This is indeed so, as leaders are distinct from managers though a single person may embody both roles. Kotter (as cited in Clawson, 2006) noted, "Management is about coping with complexity, and leadership is about coping with change" (p. 382). Change is not about a plan per se (management) but about how one executes such a plan (vision). Vision is the distinguishing characteristic of a leader. Kotter (as cited in Clawson, 2006) noted that "Great vision emerges when a powerful mind, working long and hard on massive amounts of information, is able to see ... interesting patterns and new possibilities" (p. 382).

I will demonstrate the foregoing by examining four leadership theories; situational, contingency, transactional, and transformational, how they contrast with each other, and the effects they may have on contemporary leadership issues.

Situational Leadership

Hersey and Blanchard (as cited in Wren, 1995) described situational leadership as "a way of adapting leadership behaviors to features of the situation and the followers" (p. 210). This theory is another in the continuum of attempts to identify and define leadership characteristics. First, leaders were born not made, according to the great man theory. Then the emphasis on leadership theory shifted to examining traits. This theory states that leaders have leadership characteristics not possessed by followers. Chemers (as cited in Wren, 1995) noted, "The objective of the research was to identify specifically what unique features of the individual was associated with leadership" (p. 84). Third, the focus shifted to behaviors. Chemers (as cited in Wren, 1995) noted that "These researchers trained graduate research assistants in behaviors indicative of the three leadership styles: autocratic, democratic, and laissez-faire" (p. 84).

Hershey and Blanchard (as cited in Wren, 1995,) not convinced by the existing evidence, proceeded to "demonstrate the appropriate relationship between leader's behavior and a particular aspect of the situation – the readiness level exhibited by the followers" (p. 207). This approach to leadership "pays special attention to contextual factors: the nature of the work performed by the leader's unit, the individual characteristics of the followers, or the nature of the external environment" (Clawson, 2006, p. 386). The theory makes a relationship between followers' readiness levels on a scale of R1 to R4 and the leader's task and relationship behavior on a scale of S1 to S4. The combination of these two sets of characteristics will dictate whether the leader plays the role of delegating, participating, selling, or telling.

McLaurin (2006) noted that "Situational leadership theory (SLT) asserts that there is no one best style of leadership or way to influence people. The leader needs to respond to the situation with appropriate task and relationship behavior based on followers' readiness" (p. 101). The leader-follower relationship and how followers accept his or her vision will determine the leader's effectiveness.

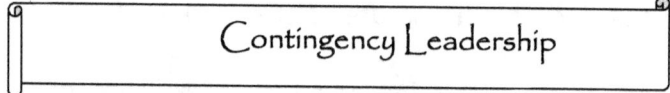

Contingency Leadership

Fred Feidler's work on his least preferred co-worker (LPC) scale may be seen as the launch of contingency leadership. In his 15 years study, Feidler (as cited in Wren, 1995) noted that "certainty, predictability, and control" influence situations. He developed the situational control scale influenced by leader-member relations, task structure, and position power. He argued that these three factors "dictate a leader's situational control" (Bolden, Gosling, Marturano, & Dennison, 2003, p. 9). Contingency theory therefore extends or refines situational theory notably in arguing that situational variables influences appropriate actions leaders take given prevailing circumstances.

In contemporary relations, followers are eager to participate in decision-making as leaders' roles are constantly expanding. Empowering followers will motivate them to achieve objectives and meet deadlines while leaders are able to use their time more constructively. Yun, Cox, and Sims (2006) noted, "By empowering followers, leaders enlist the aid of many to cope with uncertainty beyond their own limits" (p. 375).

Transactional Leadership

In analyzing earlier theories of leadership like those preceding this sections, Burns found that empirical data did not substantially support these earlier theories. In his book Leadership, Burns introduced the concept of transforming leadership. Burns (as cited in Bolden, Gosling, Marturano, and Dennison, 2003) noted that transforming leadership "is a relationship of mutual stimulation and elevation that converts followers into leaders and may convert leaders into moral agents" (p. 14). Bass and Avolio (as cited in Loahavichien, Fredendall and Cantrell, 2009) noted that transactional leadership is used to "produce incremental change" (p. 8).

Zagorsek, Dimovski, and Skerlavaj (2009) proffered, "The transactional leadership process builds upon exchange: the leader offers rewards ... for the performance of desired behaviors and the completion of certain tasks" (p. 147). Transactional leadership is therefore about influencing compliance of followers with incentives that alter behavior. Transactional leadership seems lacking in vision that results in the absence of trust, enthusiasm, and loyalty. It would appear that rewards are the sole motivating factor affecting results. Empowered followers are more attuned to leadership demands in a contemporary dispensation.

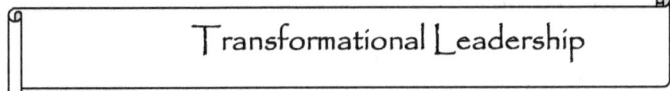

Transformational Leadership

Baas, building upon Burns earlier work on transforming leadership, conceptualized transformational leadership. Transformational leadership "was viewed as the type of leadership needed to create radical change" (Laohavichien et al., 2009, p. 8). Yukl (as cited in Avolio and Yammarino, 2008) defined transformational leadership "as transforming the values and priorities of followers and motivating them to perform beyond their expectations" (p. 69). In the context of today's organizations when followers expect to be equals in participation, engagement, trust, mutual respect, responsibility, and authority, transformational leadership would seem the most appropriate leadership style to create a "best fit" within contemporary organizational structure. Zagorsek, Dimovski, and Skerlavaj (2009) noted, "Transformational leaders encourage open, honest, and timely communication, and foster dialogue and collaboration between team members" (p. 148).

Transformational leadership engages followers in analysis, interpretation, decision, and action. This approach to leadership provides the strongest leader-follower coherence and motivation and by such virtue is a results oriented method. Couto (as cited in Wren, 1995) noted that Baas sees transformational leadership as producing "entrepreneurial champions, organizational champions, and champions of radical military innovations" (p. 105). From the analysis presented, these conclusions by Bass should not seem distant or unattainable.

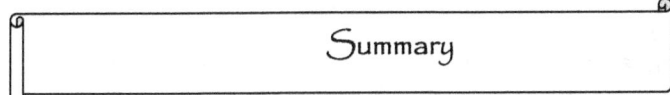

Summary

Kotter (as cited in Clawson, 2006) noted that leadership is "the process of moving a group (or groups) in some direction through mostly noncoercive means" (p. 382). Good leadership must be the hallmark of leaders hoping to maximize results without enslaving their followers. Business leaders, especially in times of trying circumstances, should reach within their souls and discover their inner abilities to give the best guidance, motivation, and influence to attain success. Kouzes (as cited in Jossey-Bass, 2003) noted, "Leadership is an observable set of skills and abilities" (p. xvii). He also

stated, "Leadership is a relationship between those who

aspire to lead and those who choose to follow" (p. xvii).

The onus is on the leader to analyze each leadership styles,

discover congruence or convergence, and act

appropriately. Leaders should eliminate any extenuating

circumstances that hinder effective leadership.

Effectiveness could be seen as "the leader's contribution

to the quality of the group processes, as perceived by

followers or by outside observers" (Yukl, n.d., p. 10).

References

Avolio, B. J., & Yammarino, F. J. (Eds.). (2008).

    Transformational and charismatic leadership: The

    road ahead (1st ed.). Howard House, Bingley, UK:

    Emerald Group Publishing Limited.

Bolden, R., Gosling, J., Marturano, A., & Dennison, P.

    (2003). A review of leadership theory and

    competency frameworks. *Centre for Leadership*

    Studies, University of Exeter. Retrieved February

    26, 2010. Retrieved from http://www.leadership-

    studies.com/documents/mgmt_standards.pdf

Clawson, J. G. (2006). *Level three leadership: Getting*

    below the surface (3rd ed.). Upper Sadele River,

    NJ: Pearson Prentice Hall.

Jossey-Bass. (2003). *Business leadership*. San Francisco,

    CA: Author.

Laohavichien, T., Fredendall, L. D., & Cantrell, R. S. (2009). The effects of transformational and transactional leadership on quality improvement. *The Quality Management Journal, 16*(2), 7-24. Retrieved February 23, 2010. Retrieved from ProQuest database.

McLaurin, J. R. (2006). The role of situation in the leadership process: A review and application. *Academy of Strategic Management Journal, 5*, 97-114. Retrieved February 23, 2010. Retrieved from ProQuest database.

McLaurin, J. R. (2008). Developing an understanding of charismatic and transformational leadership. *Allied Academics International Conference. Academy of Organizational Culture, Communications and Conflict. Proceedings, 13*(2), 15-19. Retrieved February 23, 2010. Retrieved from ProQuest database.

Wren, J. T. (Ed.). (1995). *The leader's companion.* New York, N.Y.: Simon & Schuster Inc..

Yukl, G. (n.d.). *Leadership in organizations* (6th ed.). Upper Saddle River, NJ: Pearson Prentice Hall.

Yun, S., Cox, J., & Sims, H. P. (2006). The forgotten followers: a contingency model of leadership and follower self-leadership. *Journal of Managerial Psychology: Self-leadership, 21*(4), 374-388. Retrieved February 26, 2010. Retrieved from ProQuest database.

Zagorsek, H., Dimovski, V., & Skerlavaj, M. (2009). Transactional and transformational leadership impacts on organizational learning. *Journal for East Euporean Management Studies, 14*(2), 144-165. Retrieved February 23, 2010. Retrieved from ProQuest database.

Leadership has long been a complex issue to grasp, yet the very notion of leadership continues to fascinate scholars and practitioners alike. Scholars envision a need to theorize a comprehensive concept of leadership whereas practitioners endeavor to rationalize their daily experiences. "Leadership is a relationship between those who aspire to lead and those who choose to follow" (Jossey-Bass, 2003, p. xix). The scholar practitioner approach to leadership however, seeks to address confluence between theory and practice. For a practitioner therefore, leadership is "congruent upon such factors as the situation, the people, the task, the organization, and other environmental variables" (Bolden, Gosling, Marturano, & Dennison, 2003, p. 8). In this regard, leadership is about a team. "Effective leadership is defined as leadership that produces movements in the long-term best interest of the group(s) (Clawson, 2006, p. 382).

Table 1: Pearson Prentice Hall Self-Assessment Test Scores for Collaborative Team Work

	Leader A	Leader B	Leader C
Building and Leading a Team:			
- Score	106	78	99
Leadership Style:			
- People Concern	10	6	7
- Task Concern	16	9	3
Preferred Conflict-Handling Style:			
- Competing	11	10	6
- Collaborating	19	15	20
- Avoiding	8	10	14
- Accommodating	17	16	18
- Compromising	18	13	18
Preferred Type of Power:			
- Reward	4	4	3
- Coercive	1.5	1.2	1
- Legitimate	5	4	4
- Expert	5	4.5	4.7
- Referent	5	4.5	4.7

The Pearson Prentice Hall Self-Assessment tools are ideal for assisting members in assessing their fit for teamwork and collaborative learning. Take for example, *Leader C* from **Table 1** above and analyze his contribution to a team based on his test scores.

Leader C's contribution to building a team is within the top quartile of forming, conforming, storming, and performing. He is managing at the performing stage. At this stage of performance, the group manages its assigned tasks effectively, without conflict, and without the need for constant supervision. "Roles become flexible and functional, and group energy is channeled into the tasks. Structural issues have been resolved, and structure can now become supportive of task performance" (Wren, 1995, p. 359).

His leadership style is laissez-faire in that he regards people's concern as having a higher priority than the tasks undertaken. This behavior works well where group members are experienced in tackling assigned tasks and do not need constant supervision. Bolden, Gosling, Marturano, and Dennison (2003) noted that "As the followers begin to move into an above average level of maturity, the leader should decrease not only task behaviour but also relationship behaviour" (p. 10). A laissez-faire leader working with a mature set of followers will not sacrifice productivity for leadership.

Leader C's conflict-style is essentially situational. According to Yukl (n.d.) "the situation is most favorable for the leader when relations with subordinates are good, the leader has substantial position power, and the task is highly structured" (p. 216). He will therefore avoid trivial and emotional conflicts or assertiveness where such actions do not provide reasonable solutions. Wherever necessary however, he will take resolute decisions. He is particularly strong at collaborating, accommodating, compromising, and avoiding conflict.

As regards his preferred power style; legitimate, expert, and referent power seem to be his favorite style of leadership. Legitimate power is inherent in one's role in the organization. Expert power is derived from training and experience within a particular discipline. Referent power is formed from interpersonal relationships with subordinates (Wren, 1995). He is neutral to reward power and avoids coercive power. From a management perspective, he remains neutral on reward power, strong on legitimate power and avoids coercive powers.

Conclusion

Leadership is not about an individual but an "observable set of skills and abilities" (Jossey-Bass, 2003, p. xvii). Leadership is a relationship that encompasses traits, behaviors, and situations. Leadership success is therefore contingent upon many factors. No reasonable scholar can argue therefore, that there exists a preferred style of leadership. McLaurin (2006) noted "there is no one best style of leadership or way to influence people.

"The leader needs to respond to the situation with appropriate tasks and relationship behavior based on followers' readiness" (p. 101). Effective leadership therefore, is about "the leader's contribution to the quality of group process, as perceived by followers or by outside observers" (Yukl, n.d., p. 10). Effective leadership is about meeting and exceeding organizational objectives. The onus is on the leader to provide leadership. The leader must therefore meet the group's expectation or change them (McFadden, Eakin, Beck-Frazier, & McGlone, 2005) in order to be a worthy leader.

References

Bolden, R., Gosling, J., Marturano, A., & Dennison, P.

(2003). A review of leadership theory and

competency frameworks. *Centre for Leadership*

Studies, University of Exeter. Retrieved February

26, 2010. Retrieved from http://www.leadership-

studies.com/documents/mgmt_standards.pdf

Clawson, J. G. (2006). *Level three leadership: Getting*

below the surface (3rd ed.). Upper Sadele River,

NJ: Pearson Prentice Hall.

Jossey-Bass. (2003). *Business leadership*. San Francisco,

CA: Author.

McFadden, C., Eakin, R., Beck-Frazier, S., & McGlone, J.

(2005). Major approaches to the study of leadership.

Academic Exchange Quarterly, 71-75. Retrieved

February 29, 2010. Retrieved from Gale

PowerSearch database.

McLaurin, J. R. (2006). The role of situation in the

leadership process: A review and application.

Academy of Strategic Management Journal, *5*, 97-

114. Retrieved February 23, 2010. Retrieved from

ProQuest database.

Wren, J. T. (Ed.). (1995). *The leader's companion.* New

York, N.Y.: Simon & Schuster Inc..

Yukl, G. (n.d.). *Leadership in organizations* (6th ed.).

Upper Saddle River, NJ: Pearson Prentice Hall.

3 Reflective Leadership Plan

Leadership has long been a challenge to both understand and master. For centuries leadership has intrigued scholars but only fairly recently leadership has got so munch focus in the social sciences. Bass (as cited in Wren, 1995) noted, "Leadership is one of the world's oldest preoccupations" (p. 49). Chemers (as cited in Wren, 1995) proffered that studying leadership scientifically started around 1910. Chemers spoke about three periods of leadership culminating in its current contemporary view that started during the 1960s to present.

This keen interest in leadership has a fundamental basis in deciphering its effectiveness. Burns noted that humans crave for compelling leadership (Wren, 1995, p. 27). Both organizations and nations want to understand what exemplify and distinguish their great leaders' effectiveness. Effectiveness comes through achieving expectations or being visionary enough to change such expectations. "Since leadership is related to fulfilling the expectations of a group, leaders must either meet these expectations or change them" (McFadden, Eakin, Beck-Frazier, & McGlone, 2005, p. 72). Clawson (2006) posited that effective leadership produce results best suited for the long-term benefit of the group (p. 382). He further noted that the process of leadership is about taking the group in a particular direction without being coercive. How one may endeavor to achieve such noble means is my focus for leadership in the pursuing paragraphs.

Your Reflective Leadership Plan

Always be prepared for the challenges of the particular sector in which you are engaged. Endeavor to glean the necessary attitudes and behavior that will assist you to have a positive effect on human and social conditioning. Build an understanding to be discerning as you journey through the complex and often confusing matrix of effective leadership.

Base arguments on merits supported by facts. Understand the role abstraction plays in synthesis and analysis. Kiley (2009) noted that "threshold concepts are concepts that are so critical to an understanding of the discipline that advanced disciplinary learning" (p. 297). Aitchison and Lee (2006) proffered that:

> Research student writers, preoccupied with the complexity of the writing process, are often concerned *simultaneously* [italics added] with the major questions of thinking, learning, knowing, engaging, positioning, becoming and writing that constitute their extended experience of research

degree candidature and their transaction with the thesis text (p. 268).

Recognize the importance of teamwork and group members' skills. D'Andrea-O'Brien and Bono posited that:

True team learning is the ability of members to share and build on their individual knowledge so that their collective knowledge enables them to continually improve team and organization performance as well as to discover, develop and implement completely new ways of doing business (p. 5).

In working with teams however, a leader must be mindful that the preferred characteristics are emphasized. Group members should be cooperative, collaborative, disciplined, innovative, and critical. Being critical plays a very important role. Sometimes to act as devil's advocate helps with the group's effectiveness. The Bay of Pigs saga could have been avoided if President Kennedy had minimized the effect of groupthink (Wren, 1995, p. 360). Drach-Zahavy and Somech (2001) noted that "innovation is related to intentional attempts of team members to arrive at anticipated benefits for the individual, the team, the organization, or the surrounding society" (p. 111). These are all changes that one can effect immediately and refine over time.

I would encourage you to look back at chapter two and, in particular, the Pearson Prentice Hall Self-assessment tests. Visit their library and take the tests. These tests are immensely important to understanding self and by extension, seeking better management skills and leadership abilities. Leadership is a complex issue and time must be invested in the requisite knowledge for proper management, direction, and control. To lack these skill-sets is to render you incapable of effective leadership.

References

Aitchison, C., & Lee, A. (2006). Research writing:

problems and pedagogies. *Teaching in Higher*

Education, 11(3), 265-278. Retrieved February 8,

2010. doi:10.1080/13562510600680574

Clawson, J. G. (2006). *Level three leadership: Getting*

below the surface (3rd ed.). Upper Sadele River,

NJ: Pearson Prentice Hall.

Drach-Zahavy, A., & Somech, A. (2001). Understanding

team innovation: The role of team processes and

structures. *Group Dynamics: Theory, Research, and*

Practice, 5(2), 111-123. Retrieved January 25,

2010. doi:10.1037/1089-2699.5.2.111

D'Andrea-O'Brien, C., & Buono, A. F. (1996). Building

effective learning teams: Lessons from the field..

SAM Advanced Management Journal, 61(3), 4-9.

Retrieved January 18, 2010. Retrieved from

EBSCOhost database.

Kiley, M. (2009). Identifying treshold concepts and

proposing strategies to support doctoral candidates.

Innovations in Education & Teaching International,

46(3), 293-304. Retrieved February 8, 2010.

Retrieved from EBSCOhost database.

McFadden, C., Eakin, R., Beck-Frazier, S., & McGlone, J.

(2005). Major approaches to the study of leadership.

Academic Exchange Quarterly, 71-75. Retrieved

February 29, 2010. Retrieved from Gale

PowerSearch database.

Wren, J. T. (Ed.). (1995). *The leader's companion.* New

York, N.Y.: Simon & Schuster Inc..

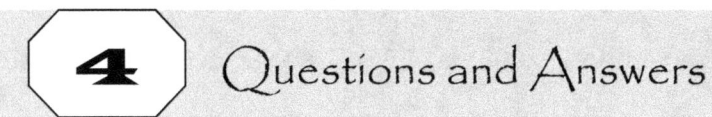

4 Questions and Answers

Can a Person of Average Charisma
or Personality be a Superior Leader?

Leadership is about leaders meeting expectations of others whereas effective leadership lies within meeting those expectations or changing them (McFadden, Eakin, Beck-Frazier, & McGlone, 2005, p. 72). Therefore, leadership is not about any particular trait or even style. Successful leaders are contingent upon "those who can adapt their leader behavior to meet the needs of their followers and the particular situation" (Wren, 1995, p. 148).

Charismatic theories, an emotional approach to leadership, ascribe that such leadership "arises from the interaction of leader capacities, leader behavior, follower characteristics, and situational factors" (Avolio &

Yammarino, 2008, p. 257). Other extensions to such theories may include providing more effective intrinsic values such as collective responsibilities, recognizing followers' abilities, providing meaningful rewards for accomplished goals, inspiration, and personal commitment by the leader (Avolio & Yammarino). These characteristics all contribute to a leader's success. The leader must therefore, study the plethora of divergent and contending factors, assess his or her strengths and the strengths of followers, and keep abreast of the situational ramifications so that meaningful, timely, and relevant decisions can be made.

As noted by Fielder and Chemers (as cited in McFadden, Eakin, Beck-Frazier, and McGlone, 2005), it is unwise to try to change leadership to suite a particular situation, instead, one should try to "place leaders into positions that match their leadership style" (p. 73). When leaders of average charisma or personality are placed in "best-fit" situations, it is highly likely that the result of that leadership will be successful.

When transformational leaders, those most endowed with charisma, can "encourage open, honest, and timely communications, and foster dialogue and collaboration between team members" (Zagorsek, Dimovski, & Skerlavaj, 2009, p. 148,) those empowered leaders are likely to succeed irrespective of the specific traits of the leader. When a leader recognizes his or her faults or weaknesses, the leader may empower others, especially those he or she trust with certain tasks and responsibilities. "By empowering followers, leaders enlist the aid of the many to cope with uncertainty beyond their own limits. In addition, followers have flexibility to engage their own ability more fully to help the organization enhance competitiveness" (Yun, Cox, & Sims, 2006, p.

375). Leadership is about the success of the entire team and not just of the leader. If the leader can achieve all these endeavors, the leader would have succeeded at leadership notwithstanding his or her particular weaknesses.

References

Avolio, B. J., & Yammarino, F. J. (Eds.). (2008).

   Transformational and charismatic leadership: The

   road ahead (1st ed.). Howard House, Bingley, UK:

   Emerald Group Publishing Limited.

McFadden, C., Eakin, R., Beck-Frazier, S., & McGlone, J.

   (2005). Major approaches to the study of leadership.

   Academic Exchange Quarterly, 71-75. Retrieved

   February 29, 2010. Retrieved from Gale

   PowerSearch database.

Wren, J. T. (Ed.). (1995). *The leader's companion.* New

   York, N.Y.: Simon & Schuster Inc..

Yun, S., Cox, J., & Sims, H. P. (2006). The forgotten

   follower: a contingency model of leadership and

   follower self-leadership. *Journal of Managerial*

   Psychology: Self-leadership, 21(4), 374-388.

Retrieved February 27, 2010. Retrieved from

ProQuest database.

Zagorsek, H., Dimovski, V., & Skerlavaj, M. (2009).

Transactional and transformational leadership

impacts on organizational learning. *Journal for East*

Euporean Management Studies, *14*(2), 144-165.

Retrieved February 23, 2010. Retrieved from

ProQuest database.

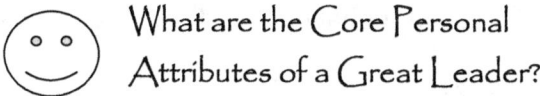 What are the Core Personal
Attributes of a Great Leader?

In earlier dispensations, between the 19th and early 20th centuries, great leaders were presumed to be born, not trained. Such leaders were endowed with certain universal traits. The universality of the traits these leaders possess attributed to their greatness. This early phenomenon the "great man" theory evolved into what is known as trait theory some time during the 20th century. This resulted from the fact that such earlier behaviors became outdated and inflexible, inhibiting the growth of organizations (Wren, 1995, p. 134).

Great investments were put into trait theory to establish the correlations between traits and their universal appeal. Researchers discovered that traits do matter but not necessarily in a universal context, as leadership was not solely driven by innate characteristics, but also by individuals' behavior and the situations existing at the time between followers and leaders. Leadership is "contingent upon such factors as the situation, the people, the task, the organization, and other environmental variables" (Bolden, Gosling, Marturano, & Dennison, 2003, p. 8). Notwithstanding, a great deal of effort went into studying the effect of charisma on leadership (Bolden et al., p. 7).

In these contemporary times, most followers are unwilling to follow blindly behind their leaders. Followers demand empowerment. Followers want to participate in decision-making and output. Today's leaders must be able to "encourage open, honest, and timely communication, and foster dialogue and collaboration between teams" (Zagorsek, Dimovski, & Skerlavaj, 2009, p. 148). Today's leaders must therefore, be able to adapt to a multiplicity of skills and abilities to be effective at leadership.

Leadership Core Attributes

"Leadership is an observable set of skills and abilities" (Jossey-Bass, 2003, p. XVII). Followers therefore pay a great deal of attention to their leaders. The first attribute must therefore be credibility. "Credibility is the foundation of leadership" (Jossey-Bass, p. xix). A leader must display competence. The leader must be able to adjust behaviors and though process according to the situations encountered. (Oyinlade, 2006, p. 26). Further, Oyinlade (2006) noted that a leader should have the abilities to:

> motivate others, to provide support for subordinates, to listen well, to have knowledge of his/her organization, to have vision, to have good interpersonal skills, to be able to resolve conflicts, to have knowledge of the law, to be able to

establish directions for others, as well as align people toward common directions (p. 26).

Other characteristics may include strategic opportunism, globally adapted, data analyst, adaptable across organizations, community builder, multitasking, being able to influence followers to lead, and possess good communication skills (p. 26).

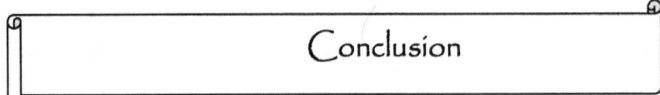

Conclusion

It may be difficult to enumerate the exact core values of leaders because leaders do have their own leadership styles and modus operandi. An effective way of improving leadership therefore, is to place leaders in positions more suitable for their styles. (McFadden, Eakin, Beck-Frazier, & McGlone). Nevertheless, the characteristics enumerated may be treated as applicable attributes for sound and effective leadership.

References

Bolden, R., Gosling, J., Marturano, A., & Dennison, P.

   (2003). A review of leadership theory and

   competency frameworks. *Centre for Leadership*

   Studies, University of Exeter. Retrieved February

   26, 2010. Retrieved from http://www.leadership-

   studies.com/documents/mgmt_standards.pdf

Jossey-Bass. (2003). *Business leadership*. San Francisco,

   CA: Author.

McFadden, C., Eakin, R., Beck-Frazier, S., & McGlone, J.

   (2005). Major approaches to the study of leadership.

   Academic Exchange Quarterly, 71-75. Retrieved

   February 29, 2010. Retrieved from Gale

   PowerSearch database.

Oyinlade, A. O. (2006). A method of assessing leadership

   effectiveness: Introducing the essential behavioral

   leadership qualities approach. *Performance*

Improvement Quarterly, *19*(1), 25-40. Retrieved

March 8, 2010. Retrieved from ProQuest database.

Wren, J. T. (Ed.). (1995). *The leader's companion*. New

York, N.Y.: Simon & Schuster Inc..

Zagorsek, H., Dimovski, V., & Skerlavaj, M. (2009).

Transactional and transformational leadership

impacts on organizational learning. *Journal for East*

Euporean Management Studies, *14*(2), 144-165.

Retrieved February 23, 2010. Retrieved from

ProQuest database.

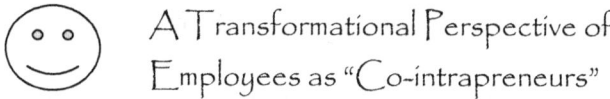# A Transformational Perspective of Employees as "Co-intrapreneurs"

Within the context of a globally competitive environment, leaders and followers alike must attune behavior and discipline to meet the resulting challenges that emanate from global competition. Coupled with the global demands for competitiveness are the need for organizational performance and output. Leaders and followers must understand this rapid transformation from industrial economies to knowledge-based service oriented economies (Wunderer, 2001). Wunderer (2001) proffered that to satisfy this new dispensation, leaders will have to seek new ways of doing things, engender new models based on team designs, decentralization, and coordination. In analyzing this transformative process, the following five elements; goals, context, potential, co-ordination, and policies will be used.

We cannot ignore the transformational leader's four core behaviors: individualized consideration, intellectual stimulation, inspirational motivation, and idealized influence in the analysis (Sosik, Potosky, & Jung, 2002). The transformational leader should use these behaviors to affect goals, context, potential, co-ordination, and policies.

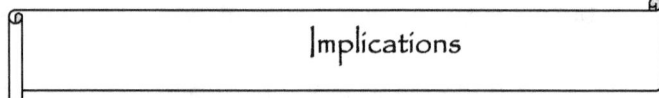

Implications

Wunderer (2001) posited that:

Entrepreneurship can be defined as the process of eliciting or evoking value from new and unique combinations or re-arrangements of resources in an uncertain and ambiguous environment. Consequently, internal entrepreneurs can be understood as co-operating organization members, which innovate, identify and create business opportunities, assemble and co-ordinate new combinations or arrangements of resources to yield or enhance value.

In this new dispensation, the *goal* for organizations is to recruit and promote not on the basis of stakeholders investments but in the long term interest of the organization. Wunderer (2001) argued that leaders must understand and properly align corporate principles and every day behaviors. Leaders must pay attention to *context*. Contexts such as the increasing demand from global competition and shifts in cultural attitudes impinge upon organizational leadership. Workers *potential* can easily be ignored if the traditional modus operandi is strictly adhered to. Schumpeter (as cited in Wunderer, 2001) proffered that "creativity alone could easily end in daydreaming ... he considers the central criteria for his entrepreneurial concept to be the ability and motivation to implement by persuading and enforce new solutions to problems" (p. 196). Division of labor abounds in such organization, co-operation and teamwork becomes essential to survival and success. Such noble ideals will be impossible without proper *co-ordination* between the contending parts. Finally, there is the need to manage this new thrust of empowerment. *Policies* will have to be followed for organization and control of business activities. "Managers can and must provide fundamental support in necessary cases. Both senior management and the HR department are responsible for ensuring that self and on-the-job developments support the co-intrapreneurial process" (Wunderer, p. 203).

Conclusion

We are guided by the maxim of Kotler who stated that "there are three types of companies: those who make things happen, those who watch things happen, and those

who wonder what happened!" (Wunderer, 2001, p. 206).

References

Sosik, J. J., Potosky, D., & Jung, D. I. (2002). Adaptive

self-regulation: Meeting others' expectations of

leadership and performance. *The Journal of Social

Psychology, 142*(2), 211-233. Retrieved March 25,

2010. Retrieved from ProQuest database.

Wunderer, R. (2001). Employees as "co-intrapreneurs" - a

transformational concept. *Institute for Leadership

and HR Management, University of St Gallen,

22*(5), 193-211. Retrieved March 25, 2010.

Retrieved from

http://www.emeraldinsight.com.ezproxy.apollolibra

ry.com/Insight/ViewContentServlet?contentType=

Article&Filename=Published/EmeraldFullTextArtic

le/Articles/0220220501.html

 Information Literacy Influence on Scholarship, Practice, and Leadership in The Legal Industry (an example)

Whereas leadership may be the epitome to good governance, leadership does not exist in a vacuum. Good leadership demands training in various disciplines such as management, finance, project management, communication skills, tolerance, endurance, stress management, time management among a host of other interrelated disciplines. Effective leadership therefore, must be cognizant of the important roles it plays in directing, motivating, leading, and managing the affairs of firms and organizations. Good leadership must be compatible with the rationale of good governance and management styles and must be willing to face new challenges and the constant change that today's information age bring. He or she must be adaptable to the changing economic, political, social, or cultural circumstances. Information Literacy (IL) expose leaders to a better understanding of the matrices of economic models, the impact of social programs instituted by governments upon such models, the political climate and its influence upon business decisions, if governments are fairly elected, and if business decisions are affected and caused by corrupt practices.

The legal industry is an industry consisting primarily of practitioners in various disciplines of law. Such areas include criminal and civil law, intellectual property, finance, commercial, conveyance, taxation, and insolvency, to name a few. This industry is a challenging one that is affected by government laws and regulations and through customs and institutions such as churches and universities. IL has a direct effect on the industry in that such practical and scholastic exposure prepares attorneys to cope with the challenges and complexities inherent with the industry.

Information Literacy (IL) addresses "the knowledge, skills and understanding essential for the effective location, assessment and use of information, in all forms, necessary to meet the wide range of needs that arise in people's lives" (Shenton, 2009, p. 20). Shenton (2009) went on to speak about the need to find relevant and timely information and the paradox that such relevance may entail. For example, when universities limit students to sources of information deem reliable, students accept the information without much thought and therefore, students are less likely to develop their critical thinking skills. Whereas, if students were allowed to source information outside the body of data deemed appropriate, students are more likely to question the data's validity, and to exercise critical thinking upon the data gleaned.

Shenton (2009) pointed out that when learners are not challenged through research assignments appropriate to demand the IL skill; their critical thinking skills remain underdeveloped. Critical thinking is a prerequisite for every attorneys and paralegal individual as it is for every manager and leader.

It should be clear how scholarly, experienced leadership modeled to the benefit of an ever-changing and knowledgeable world. A tested and proven way to achieve this balance between scholarship and practice is to apply the scholar, practitioner, leader model enunciated by University of Phoenix (UOPX). When leaders bring their experience and knowledge together such as carrying out any necessary research, analyzing data and facts, and assessing the circumstances surrounding the problem, they are likely to make thorough, informed, and applicable decisions to the problems they are addressing. Humans have a right to empowerment and happiness and will muster the courage to challenge any difficulties the information era brings. To be effective, especially in an industry such as law, one must be able to distinguish facts from fiction. One must do the requisite research to obtain the relevant set of information. Persons must know that they know or that they do not know and, if so, where to ascertain the information needed. IL equips a leader with the requisite knowledge and skill-sets he or she need to be an effective leader. "Information Literacy, therefore, is a means of personal empowerment" (Presidential committee, 1989, ¶ 6).

The influence of IL on scholarship, practice, and leadership formulate the very essence of society's political culture. It influences society's democratic way of life. The information literate individual, for example, will know that when carrying out research and development, his or her first option is to do a feasibility study of the current situation. He or she will try to establish whether there is substantial information of value, see if production cost is manageable, find out if the project is feasible, make sure there is a reasonable return on investment, and that the good or service can enter the market in a timely manner. All these are important issues that deserve thorough research early in the development stage of the life cycle of the invention or creation. "When the technical librarian for an electronics firm was asked to do a literature search for one of its engineers, four people had already been working to resolve a problem for more than a year" (Presidential committee, 1989, ¶ 11). Had the appropriate research been done prior to the engineers investing so much effort and finance in their project, it would be obvious that a solution exist. This would result in valuable time and cost savings to the company pursuing the research.

Influence that comes to the industry from advanced training can help the success rate of the individual firms and therefore increase the success rate of the industry. Here again, it is the ability to manage the plethora of data available to ascertain the required information that will give the distinct advantage to "council." IL can heavily influence the scholar, practitioner, leader model. This could be achieved through the greater involvement of active librarians influencing the scholastic syllabus and collaborating more with academia. Too often, without the benefit of IL, the researcher does not properly evaluate information for its accuracy or its validity. Unsubstantiated sources are often taken for granted at face value. This tends to be so because of the lack of IL skills and therefore the absence of both planning and problem-solving abilities. Far truer however, is that with the absence of IL skills, the researcher is more likely to treat the research parochially. The learner seems to think only in his or her own corner. This is an outdated approach especially in an era when the world is a single global village. Globalization and the use of the Internet make it obsolete for leaders to think in these isolated terms. Such a leader is uncompetitive and will lead his or her company into bankruptcy. Lauer and Yodanis (2004) found that "in an increasingly interdependent world, most if not all major issues acquire worldwide dimensions and require global solutions" (p. 304).

IL complements cross-functional disciplines in higher education. This complementary relationship bears a direct effect on one's scholarly and practical modus operandi. However, its success depends on it being "integrated, relevant, ongoing, collaborative and applied" (Zabel, 2004, ¶ 16).

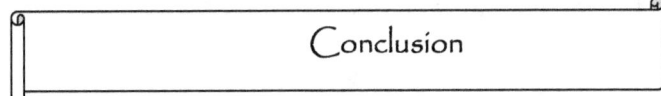

Conclusion

The legal industry is an industry that demands individuals who know how to gather relevant information for case sensitive and guided use. This industry demand leadership capable of operating at high levels while managing undue stress. Individuals in this industry have to exhibit a high aptitude for both scholarly and practical approaches to problem-solving techniques. The individual has to demonstrate leadership that can withstand the most difficult challenges while maintaining calm. A leader equipped with the skills of IL is a candidate ready for the challenge of scholarship and practice to channel resources relevant to his or her industry. The legal industry is an apt one for IL and by extension, its influence on scholarship, practice, and leadership. Notwithstanding the example being the legal industry, the argument is true for any other industry and its practitioners.

References

Lauer, S. R., & Yodanis, C. L. (2004)). The international
social survey programme (ISSP): A tool for
teaching with an international perspective. *Teaching
Sociology, 32*(3), 304-313. Retrieved January 14,
2010. Retrieved from ProQuest Education Journals.

Presidential committee on information literacy: Final
report. (1989). *American Library Association.*
Retrieved from
http://www.ala.org/ala/mgrps/divs/acrl/publications/
whitepapers/presidential.cfm

Shenton, A. K. (2009). Anew two-cultures debate:
Information literacy and school practices. *Education
Journal*(118), 20-20. Retrieved January 14, 2010.
Retrieved from EBSCOhost database.

Zabel, D. (2004). A reaction to "information literacy and
higher education". *Journal of Academic Leadership,*

30(1), 17-21. Retrieved January 14, 2010. Retrieved from EBSCOhost database.

 Leadership, Intuition, & Learning

There are two fundamental differences between leadership and management. First, leadership is *not* management. Leadership has a different focus. This distinction can be summed up in the phrase "management is about coping with complexity, and leadership is about coping with change" (Clawson, 2006, p. 382).

The distinction between complexity and change is essential to good leadership. Vision is therefore the essential characteristic of a leader. A plan of itself is a function of management. How one executes such a plan is what constitutes leadership. Kotter (as cited in Clawson, 2006) proffered that "great vision emerges when a powerful mind, working long and hard on massive amounts of information, is able to see (or recognize in suggestions from others) interesting patterns and new possibilities" (p. 382).

Second, no special type or style of leadership exists. Leadership is contingent upon certain traits, behaviors, and situations. McLaurin (2006) posited, "There is no best style of leadership or way to influence people. The leader needs to respond to the situation with appropriate tasks and relationship behavior based on followers' readiness" (p. 101). Whereas Hersey and Blanchard (as cited in Wren, 1995) proffered that successful leaders are "those who can adapt their leader behavior to meet the needs of their followers and the particular situation" (p. 148). Clawson (2006) noted that situational leadership "pays special attention to contextual factors: the nature of the work performed by the leader's unit, the individual characteristics of the followers, or the nature of the external environment" (p. 386).

Although I recognize the importance of intuition (skills gained through experience), I cannot underestimate complementing such skill-sets with formal training. To base decisions purely on intuition and ignore scholarship and practice is to be lacking in effective leadership.

References

Clawson, J. G. (2006). *Level three leadership: Getting below the surface* (3rd ed.). Upper Sadele River, NJ: Pearson Prentice Hall.

McLaurin, J. R. (2006). The role of situation in the leadership process: A review and application. *Academy of Strategic Management Journal, 5,* 97-114. Retrieved February 23, 2010. Retrieved from ProQuest database.

Wren, J. T. (Ed.). (1995). *The leader's companion.* New York, N.Y.: Simon & Schuster Inc.

 Power and its Relationship to Leadership

"Leadership is a relationship between those who aspire to lead and those who choose to follow" (Jossey-Bass, 2003, p. xix). Credibility must therefore be at the center of such relationship if there is to be effective leadership. "Credibility is the foundation of leadership" (Jossey-Bass, p. xix). A leader's credibility is necessary as inherent in leadership is the possession of power. How leaders use such power is very important to leadership style, behavior, and decisions. The Concise Oxford Dictionary (1995) defined power as "the ability to do or act, a particular faculty of body or mind, government, influence, or authority" (p. 1071). The historian and moralist Lord Acton noted, "Power tends to corrupt, and absolute power corrupts absolutely" (The Phrase Finder, n.d., p. 1). British Prime Minister William Pitt noted that

"Unlimited power is apt to corrupt the minds of those who possess it" (The Phrase Finder, p. 1). Understanding both the roles of leadership and power is therefore essential to good governance and leadership.

Psychologist Warren Bennis (as cited in Wren, 1995) noted that "power is a leader's currency, or the primary means through which leaders get things done in the organization" (p. 137). This does not mean that leaders have to be power hungry or zealots to be efficient. Effective leadership appreciates power as "something that can be created and distributed to followers without detracting from their own power" (Wren, p. 137). Zealots seek power for personal gains. Such leaders seek power as an end within itself (personalized power.) Transformational leaders however seek power "as a means to achieve goals, or a vision" (socialized power) (Wren, p. 137).

One must understand the kinds of power he or she has the potential to wield. French and Raven (as cited in McFadden, Eakin, Beck-Frazier, and McGlone, (2005) noted that there are five sources of power: (a) reward, (b) coercive (c) legitimate (d) expert and (e) referent. (p. 72). The whole purpose of leadership is to meet objectives and expectations of groups and organizations (McFadden, et. al., 2005.) Therefore, leaders must understand their power bases, the respective influences of such bases and apply power appropriately for the greater good of the group or organization. Kantian Deontologism would posit that leaders should exercise power in a universal way that is appropriate for everyone.

References

Jossey-Bass. (2003). *Business leadership.* San Francisco,

    CA: Author.

McFadden, C., Eakin, R., Beck-Frazier, S., & McGlone, J.

    (2005). Major approaches to the study of leadership.

    Academic Exchange Quarterly, 71-75. Retrieved

    February 29, 2010. Retrieved from Gale

    PowerSearch database.

The Phrase Finder, (n.d.). Power corrupts; absolute power

    corrupts absolutely. *Phrases.org.uk*. Retrieved

    March 15, 2010. Retrieved from

    http://www.phrases.org.uk/meanings/288200.html

Thompson, D. (Ed.). (1995). *The Concise Oxford*

    Dictionary (9th ed.). Oxford University Press:

    Clarendon Press.

Wren, J. T. (Ed.). (1995). *The leader's companion.* New

    York, N.Y.: Simon & Schuster Inc.

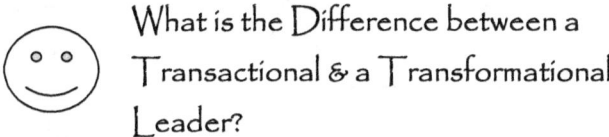

What is the Difference between a Transactional & a Transformational Leader?

Leadership has been a challenge for many centuries. It remains a mystery, although a requirement, to modern business operations and to the relationships between those responsible for directing and those responsible for executing such directions. Its mystery remains notwithstanding the plethora of studies on leadership. Although the studies continue, there exists no precise definition of what constitute leadership. Bass noted (as cited in Wren, 1995) that "the many dimensions into which leadership has been cast and their overlapping meanings have added to the confusion" (p. 38). I will examine two of the contemporary leadership theories in the following paragraphs.

Transactional Leadership

After studying earlier leadership theories like Great Man, Traits, and Behaviors; Burns was not convinced that such theories bears relevance in a contemporary world and he set out to correct the flaws that he perceived in these earlier theories. His research in this endeavor gave birth to the "transforming leader." Burns (as cited in Bolden, Gosling, Marturano, and Dennison, 2003) noted that transforming leadership "is a relationship of mutual stimulation and elevation that converts followers into leaders and may convert leaders into moral agents" (p. 14). Transactional leadership is a process between leaders and followers that entails a mutual exchange of some sort, be it salary, incentives, goods or services, and that such exchange are mutually binding. Therefore, if a follower refuses to carry out his portion of the contract then the penalties attached are applied. If the follower carries out his responsibilities as assigned, then the natural reward is the gratification promised.

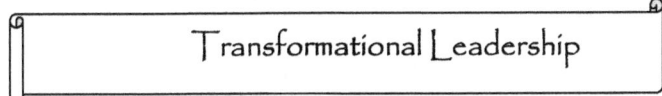

Transformational Leadership

Although transactional leadership was relevant in the last century, it has outlived it useful life and should be replaced with a timely and more relevant style of leadership appropriate to today's business environment. Today's followers yearn for empowerment and participation in the daily activities of a business. If businesses are to be successful, business leaders have to pay attention to the demands of their followers. Transformational leaders must therefore "encourage open, honest, and timely communication, and foster dialogue and collaboration between team members" (Zagorsek, Dimovski, & Skerlavaj, 2009, p. 148).

Transformational leadership is an enhanced democratic transactional leader transforming from a leader who merely provide management to one that provides vision. It is this vision that most clearly distinguishes a transformational leader from a transactional leader. Cuto (as cited in Wren, 1995) noted that Bass understand transformational leadership as creating "entrepreneurial champions, organizational champions, and champions of radical military innovations" (p. 105).

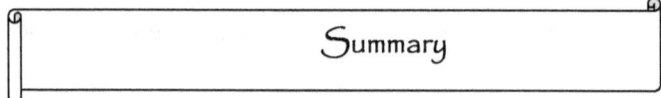

Summary

Whereas transactional leadership has served its time, transformational leadership empowers followers to participate actively in the decision-making process and gives such followers ownership of the decisions they make.

Followers are likely to buy into the actions emanating from

such results and are likely to contribute more effectively to

successful business operations.

References

Bolden, R., Gosling, J., Marturano, A., & Dennison, P. (2003). A review of leadership theory and competency frameworks. *Centre for Leadership Studies: University of Exeter*. Retrieved February 26, 2010. Retrieved from http://www.leadership-studies.com/documents/mgmt_standards.pdf

Wren, J. T. (Ed.). (1995). *The leader's companion*. New York, N.Y.: Simon & Schuster Inc..

Zagorsek, H., Dimovski, V., & Skerlavaj, M. (2009). Transactional and transformational leadership impacts on organizational learning. *Journal for East Euporean Management Studies, 14*(2), 144-165. Retrieved February 23, 2010. Retrieved from ProQuest database.

 # Understanding the Scholar-Practitioner-Leader Model

Leadership does not exist in a vacuum. Leadership demands training in a wide range of disciplines to be effective, because its primary role is a visionary one built upon other management functions such as planning, organizing, motivating, and controlling the means of production including human capital. The scholar-practitioner-leader model is ideal for persons engaged in the industry that require scholarly aptitude to enhance their effectiveness in the practical arena.

One will not maximize the benefits of the scholar-practitioner-leader model however unless one is exposed to information literacy (IL); that is, how to sift through information to find what is timely and relevant. IL will reinforce critically thinking about facts, sources, and applicability of information to both anticipated and existing problems. In speaking about IL, Shenton (2009) stated, IL is about the "knowledge, skills and understanding essential for the effective location, assessment and use of information …" (p. 20). Shenton is strengthening the argument that there is a nexus between IL and knowledge management, an issue central to scholarly work and practical experience, and hence to leadership.

Kerr (2009) stated that "Indeed, executives need to hone their own ability to think creatively, critically and with curiosity to make business decisions that answer the right questions, manage risk, improve productivity and use workers talents effectively in an evermore global and fast-paced world" (p. 58). Leaders therefore need IL to maximize their scholarly practitioner approach to good leadership.

References

Schott Kerr, S. (2009). Critical thinking: A critical strategy

for financial executives. *Financial Executive,*

25(10), 58-61. Retrieved January 19, 2010.

Retrieved from EBSCOhost database

Shenton, A. K. (2009). Anew two-cultures debate:

Information literacy and school practices. *Education*

Journal(118), 20-20. Retrieved January 14, 2010.

Retrieved from EBSCOhost database.

 # Which is More Important: Leader or Follower?

Leadership is about motivating, inspiring, encouraging, and aligning followers to a vision espoused. Hersey and Blanchard (as cited in Wren, 1995) noted, "Successful leaders are those who can adapt their leader behavior to meet the needs of their followers and the particular situation" (p. 148). Kotter (as cited in Clawson, 2006) noted, "Management is about coping with complexity, and *leadership* [italics added] is about coping with change" (p. 382). Leadership and followership are therefore two sides of the same coin; one cannot exist without the other.

For there to be followers there must be leaders. Conversely, leaders cannot exist without followers because the purpose of the leader is to engage his or her followers in a commonly shared vision. At respective times during this relationship, there may be followers who temporarily take on the leadership role, for example, to accomplish a particular task. In that regard, the leader becomes a follower for the particular task being undertaken by the follower. Usually, leadership emerges when there is a void or an absence of vision. "Great vision emerges when a powerful mind, working long and hard on massive amounts of information, is able to see … interesting patterns and new possibilities" (Clawson, 2006, p. 382).

The foregoing is more apt in today's contemporary dispensation as leadership styles shift from dictatorial to transformational. With transformational leadership, followers must be empowered. Followers demand a piece of the pie and leaders must "encourage open, honest, and timely communication, and foster dialogue and collaboration between team members" (Zagorsek,

Dimovski, & Skerlavaj, 2009, p. 148). Today's leader-follower relationship is a team, a relationship no different from a marriage. The scope of the two may be different but the shared values, vision, and results are arguably the same. The leader-follower relationship is about collaboration, cooperation, and results. "By empowering followers, leaders enlist the aid of many to cope with uncertainty beyond their own limits" (Yun, Cox, & Sims, 2006, p. 375).

References

Clawson, J. G. (2006). *Level three leadership: Getting below the surface* (3rd ed.). Upper Sadele River, NJ: Pearson Prentice Hall.

Wren, J. T. (Ed.). (1995). *The leader's companion.* New York, N.Y.: Simon & Schuster Inc..

Yun, S., Cox, J., & Sims, H. P. (2006). The forgotten followers: a contingency model of leadership and follower self-leadership. *Journal of Managerial Psychology: Self-leadership, 21*(4), 374-388. Retrieved February 26, 2010. Retrieved from ProQuest database.

Zagorsek, H., Dimovski, V., & Skerlavaj, M. (2009). Transactional and transformational leadership impacts on organizational learning. *Journal for East Euporean Management Studies, 14*(2), 144-165.

Retrieved February 23, 2010. Retrieved from

ProQuest database.

NOTES

NOTES